For information regarding permission, please write to
Malcom Explains, LLC, Attention: Media Department, PO Box 18193,
Shreveport, LA 71118.

ISBN-13: 978-1-959101-01-7
Printed in the U.S.A.

First edition, October 2022

You Are...

Fabulous

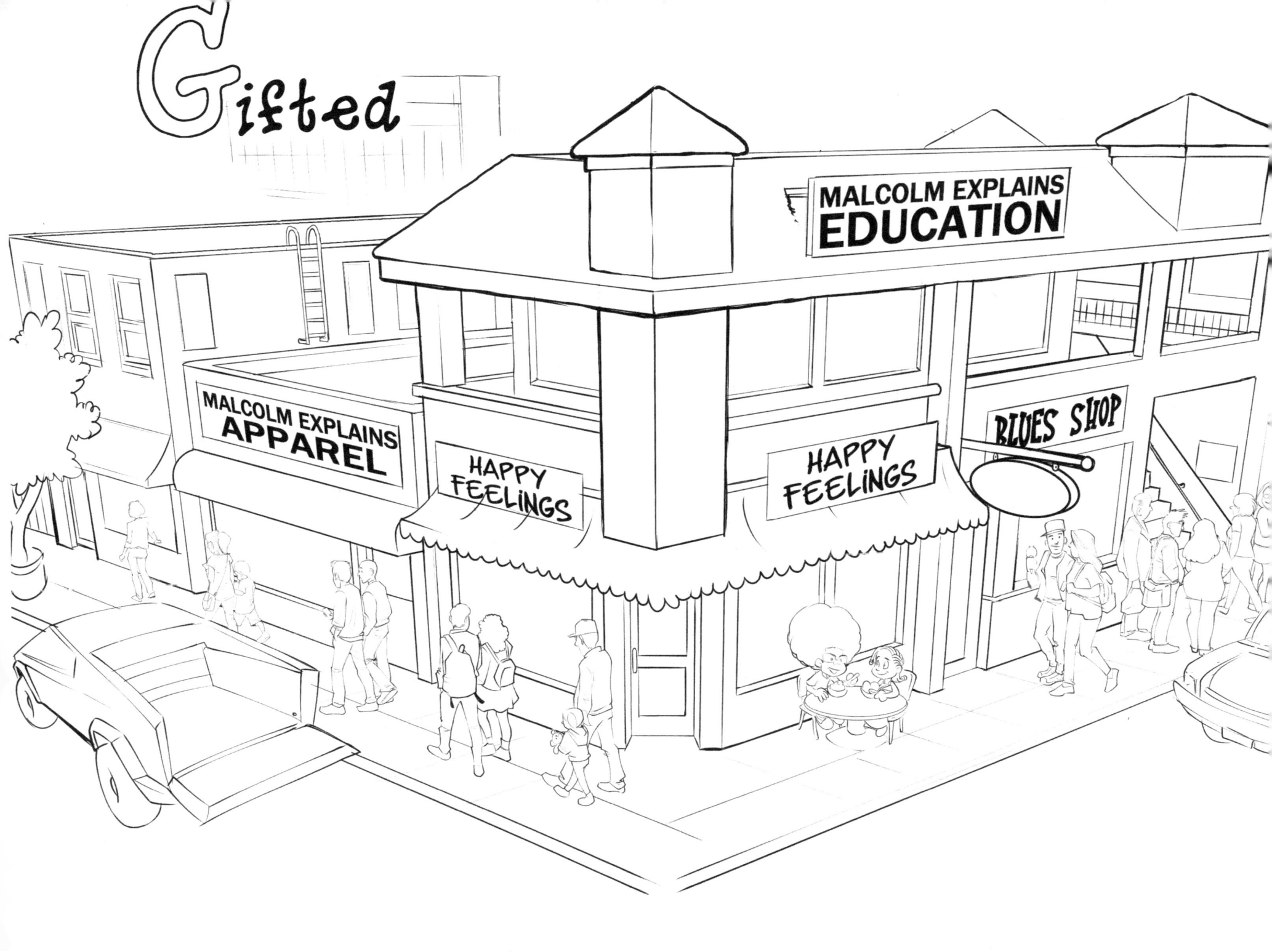

I loved

Motivated

Outstanding

Youthful

GLOSSARY

Awesome: extremely impressive.

Brave: ready to face danger, showing courage

Creative: a person with imagination and original ideas.

Dynamic: a person with a positive attitude and full of energy and new ideas.

Excellence: being outstanding or extremely good.

Fabulous: amazingly good; wonderful.

Gifted: having exceptional talent or natural ability.

Healthy: in good health.

Intelligent: showing the ability to easily learn or understand things.

Jubilant: feeling or expressing happiness and triumph.

Kind: having a friendly, generous, and considerate nature.

Loved: a deep feeling of affection.

Motivated: to inspire, drive, and encourage.

Noble: having or showing high moral principles and ideals.

Outstanding: exceptionally good.

Proud: feeling satisfied as a result of your achievements or qualities.

Quirky: having peculiar or unexpected traits.

Radiant: shining brightly; expressing love, confidence, or happiness.

Soulful: a person with a personality that is beautiful and serene.

Tactful: having an understanding and sensitivity to other's feelings.

Unique: being one of a kind and unlike anything else.

Victorious: a person who defeats an enemy or opponent.

Wholesome: promoting moral well-being.

Xenial: being nice or friendly to foreign visitors.

Youthful: young or seeming to be young.

Zealous: great energy or enthusiasm to achieve your goals